D0107361

Let us Adore Him

DRAMAS AND
MEDITATIONS
FOR ADVENT,
CHRISTMAS,
EPIPHANY

W. A. POOVEY

AUGSBURG PUBLISHING HOUSE
MINNEAPOLIS, MINNESOTA

LET US ADORE HIM

Copyright © 1972 Augsburg Publishing House

Library of Congress Catalog Card No. 72-78563

International Standard Book No. 0-8066-1229-0

Scripture quotations are from the Revised Standard Version of the Bible, copyright 1946 and 1952 by the Division of Christian Education of the National Council of Churches, and are used by permission.

All rights reserved. No part of this book may be used or reproduced in any manner whatsoever without written permission except in the case of brief quotations embodied in critical articles and reviews. For information address Augsburg Publishing House, 426 South Fifth Street, Minneapolis, Minnesota 55415.

MANUFACTURED IN THE UNITED STATES OF AMERICA

CONTENTS

Preface

Advent, Christmas, and Epiphany are great times for drama. The biblical events are certainly dramatic in themselves: the rough desert preacher John the Baptist, the promise of the Second Coming, the birth in Bethlehem, the shepherds, the Wise Men. It is perhaps significant that one of the earliest religious dramas on record is a brief scene between shepherds and a guardian at the manger.

The dramas in this book seek to explore the messages of Advent, Christmas, and Epiphany in various ways. Several dramas are biblical in setting, others are fantasies, and still others aim at realism in contemporary life. A number of the plays make use of music in one form or another, for music has been associated with this season of the year since the very first Christmas.

The Advent plays need not be presented in the order given. There is a play written for presentation at Christmas, and the Epiphany play may also be used at Christmas if desired. It was originally presented on Christmas Eve at a candlelight service. The plays have been presented at two churches in Dubuque, Iowa, Holy Trinity Lutheran and St. John's Episcopal, with casts from the two congregations. None of the plays is beyond the dramatic resources of the average congregation.

The meditations provide suggested approaches to the message of each play. The minister is free to make his own interpretation or to make no comment. Most of the plays can stand alone if desired. If the meditation is omitted, perhaps a general discussion of the message of the play during a coffee hour might be welcomed.

The title of the book suggests the goal of each play: let us adore him. The dramas should help the worshipers do that. If this happens, the material has served its purpose.

DRAMA

The Voice in the Wilderness

MEDITATION

Housecleaning Time

The Voice in the Wilderness

SETTING

The play takes place on a bare stage. No furniture is required. The play seeks to create the mood of excitement surrounding John, so the crowd must react enthusiastically, and the song must be sung with gusto.

CHARACTERS

SINGER: Either a man or a woman. Song is sung with guitar accompaniment but may be done without it if no guitarist is available.

JAPETH: fairly young, eager and enthusiastic

ADA: Japeth's wife

PHANUEL: older, a bit cynical

BEDEL: priestly spy, shrewd and wary

MALAK: another priest, younger, slightly stupid

ANNOUNCER: either a man or a woman, strong voice needed

DIAN: a young girl

JOHN THE BAPTIST: should be an imposing figure with strong voice

CROWD: Use as many as desired, men, women, and children. Must be trained so they don't get in the way of the play.

COSTUMES

The play can be done in modern dress but costumes will help. Make the costumes as simple as possible, in most cases a simple tunic will do. The garments worn by the priests must be more elaborate. John's costume should be made from burlap, and he should wear a wide leather belt. The announcer should be dressed like the rest of the characters but carry a modern microphone.

SONG

See music on page 22.

As the scene opens, the crowd enters, led by the SINGER. *Entrance can be made down the aisle.* ADA, JAPETH, *and* PHANUEL *should be in the midst of the crowd and then step away from the others when the singing ceases. The priests mingle with the crowd but do not sing. When the crowd leaves the* SINGER *may stay to lead priests in their expurgated version of the song. This can be omitted if too difficult but it helps the play, even if they sing badly.*

SINGER: There's a man in the desert.
            He is preaching every day.
            He's a prophet of the Lord,

ALL: So they say, so they say.

(Refrain)   He is John, John the Baptist,
            John the prophet of the Lord.
            Let us go, go to hear him,
            Hear his mighty stirring word.

SINGER: He is living on locusts
            And sweet honey every day,
            But his words, they are bitter,

ALL: So they say, so they say.

            (Refrain)

JAPETH: Come on, let's go out into the desert. I want to hear John preach.

ADA: Yes, we mustn't miss it. There hasn't been a prophet like that in Israel for centuries.

JAPETH: Everybody from Jerusalem is going out there. I wouldn't miss it for the world. Come on, Phanuel.

PHANUEL: Aw, I don't want to go. It's hot in the desert. And the food is terrible there. No locusts and honey for me. Besides, there's money to be made here in the temple, changing coins for the pilgrims; although you do have to pay a bribe to the high priest.

ADA: Oh Phanuel, don't be like that. You can make money some other day. You know, this John may be the Messiah.

PHANUEL: Has the high priest said so?

ADA: You know the high priest will be the last to admit that someone has come to take his place.

JAPETH: You'll just have to go, Phanuel. They say it's really a sight to see hundreds of people go into the Jordan at the same time, all confessing their sins. As a matter of fact, you could do with a bit of confessing yourself.

PHANUEL: Look who's talking. I saw you and that little dancer from Herod's court last night.

JAPETH: Be quiet. I guess we could all stand a bit of cleansing. Anyway, this John the Baptist may turn out to be a great leader. *(Whispering)* He might even lead a revolt against the Romans. Anyway, I say we should all go and listen to him preach. How about it, Phanuel?

PHANUEL: Oh, all right. I'll go. And I'll listen. But I'm not promising to take a bath in that muddy old Jordan.

ADA: Let's get going, then. The roads are already full of people. We want to get a good place close to John so we can hear what he has to say.

JAPETH: Forward, march then. Ha, ha. *(Exit singing the* REFRAIN, *crowd follows.)*

> He is John, John the Baptist,
> John the prophet of the Lord.
> Let us go, go to hear him,
> Hear his mighty, stirring word.

(Two priestly spies remain on stage, looking furtively about them.)

BEDEL: Did you hear that? The people are all fascinated by this new prophet.

MALAK: They say this John is the son of a priest.

BEDEL: That's right. His father was old Zechariah and his mother was Elizabeth. He's a child of their old age.

MALAK: Then we shouldn't have anything to worry about. He's one of us.

BEDEL: Don't be too sure. Get a crowd of yelling peasants around him and there's no telling what he may do. An enthusiastic crowd can turn the head of the wisest man. That's why the high priest wants us to go down and hear him.

MALAK: Are we supposed to arrest John, or try to stop him from preaching, or what?

BEDEL: Of course not, silly. We wouldn't have a chance with that crowd of people. They'd baptize us in the Jordan and we wouldn't come up until Judgment Day, if there is to be a Judgment Day. We're just to listen and to try to ask John some questions.

MALAK: Like what?

BEDEL: Oh, come along. I'll explain it all to you on the way. We've got to hurry or the common people will crowd around him and we'll never get near John.

MALAK: Surely the people will show respect for our priestly office.

BEDEL: You *are* an idiot. In the desert our priestly

office won't even be respected by the locusts, much less the people. Come on.

MALAK and BEDEL *(Exit, singing a partial version of the song. Singing should be mocking and sarcastic.):*

> He is John, John the Baptist,
> John the la la la la la.
> Let us go, go to hear him,
> Hear his la la la la word.

ANNOUNCER *(Runs on stage, microphone in hand):* Well, ladies and gentlemen, I wish you could be here to see the scene before us. Just below our vantage booth here I can see the River Jordan winding through the desert. Right at this spot the river is probably at its widest so there's plenty of water if people want to be baptized by this strange prophet. And it looks as if John and his disciples will need plenty of water today. There's already a large crowd gathered close to the river bank. And in every direction there seem to be more people coming all the time. Old people, young people, mothers with babies, stern looking fathers, all kinds of people. For a moment I thought I even caught a glimpse of some priests in the crowd. If I can find one I'll have a priest here with me to give you the official view from the temple rulers about John. In the meantime, let's see if we can talk to one of the pilgrims for a moment. *(Crowd has been reentering)* Young lady, young lady!

DIAN: Do you mean me?

ANNOUNCER: Yes, will you please come and talk to our listeners?

DIAN: Well, I guess it won't do any harm.

ANNOUNCER: I assure you, it won't. Would you mind telling us why you've come way out here in the desert to hear John the Baptist?

DIAN: Why I've come? Well, they say he's a true prophet. And a great preacher.

ANNOUNCER: I see. You've come to hear a prophet and the preacher.

DIAN: Not really. It's more than that. People also say this prophet knows how to bring forgiveness and peace to those who are disturbed. And that's what I'm seeking—forgiveness and peace.

ANNOUNCER: Mind telling us why?

DIAN: Oh I couldn't do that. I'd be too ashamed. But I must have help. Either I'm going to be baptized in the river, or I'm going to drown myself in it.

ANNOUNCER: You mustn't do that. But John'll help you. I'm sure he will.

DIAN: I hope so. God in heaven, how I hope so.

ANNOUNCER: Thank you. That's one of the people going to hear John the Baptist. We all wish her well. *(Enter* MALAK *and* BEDEL*)* And now here come several priests from Jerusalem. I'm sure you would all like to hear a word from one of them.

(Calling) Your excellency, your excellency.

BEDEL: Yes, what do you want?

ANNOUNCER: Simply a word from you about this new prophet. *(Moving over to* BEDEL*)* Would you mind telling me and those listening to me what the official view of the high priest is about John the Baptist?

BEDEL: No comment.

ANNOUNCER: I see. Well, perhaps you can tell us if there's been any discussion about whether this wilderness prophet might be the Messiah.

BEDEL: No comment.

ANNOUNCER: I'm sorry. Perhaps then you would be willing to give us your *personal* opinion why all these people have come out into the desert to hear this wild man who dresses in a camel's hair robe and wears a leather girdle. He's like some prophet from Israel's past. What draws men to John?

BEDEL: No comment. I must hurry to get a place close to the front of the crowd.

ANNOUNCER: *(Disgusted)* Well, thank you for a *revealing* interview. And now, friends, I think I'll move nearer too. Looks like John should be appearing in a few minutes. The crowd is getting bigger all the time. Good day to you. *(Crowd noises up and crowd begins to sing)*

CROWD: He is John, John the Baptist,
John the prophet of the Lord.
We have come, come to hear him,
Hear his mighty stirring word.

JAPETH: We want John the Baptist. Where is he?

ADA: Yes, John, come and speak to us. Preach to us, John.

CROWD: Yes. Yes. Come and preach to us, John.

PHANUEL: I've come all the way from Jerusalem. I want to see the prophet. *(John appears. A great shout goes up.)*

CROWD: Hurrah, hurrah for John the Baptist. *(John moves to center stage with crowd on either side. Crowd should react during speeches.)*

JOHN: Men and women of Israel. Many of you have come a long way to hear me today. I should be flattered by your attention. But I know I'm not important. So don't go home and tell people you have been to the Jordan and seen John the Baptist. It is my *message* that you must hear and you must remember. For I have a message from the Lord. It is this. Repent. Repent of your sins, Israel. Turn away from evil and turn again to the Lord, for the kingdom of heaven is at hand. The Lord is about to come in his power and might, and you must prepare the way for him. You must make his paths straight. You cannot greet a king in the rags of your sins. You cannot greet him with dirty hands and an evil heart. Prepare for him. The Lord must not be forced to travel over a rough road. Every valley must be filled and every mountain and hill must be brought low. The crooked must be made straight and the rough ways made smooth. Hear me, hear me, Israel. I tell you all flesh shall see the salvation of God

(*Cheers from the crowd.*) But you must repent and be ready. You must be baptized and wash away your sins.

PHANUEL: Your words burn like fire, John, son of Zechariah. But what must we do to show we are repentant?

JOHN: You must bear good fruit.

PHANUEL: How shall we do that?

JOHN: Is that so hard to understand? Let me make it plain. He that has two coats let him share with him who has none, and he who has food let him do likewise. I see some tax collectors here. If you would bear good fruits, collect no more than is your proper due. You soldiers, rob no one by violence or by false accusation and be content with your wages. Everyone, live each day as though it is your last, as though on this day you will stand before your God.

JAPETH: Hurrah for John. Let's all be baptized.

ADA: I want to be baptized too.

CROWD: Yes, yes. All of us do.

JOHN: Not all of you. I see in your midst some of the Pharisees and Sadducees from the temple. You brood of vipers, who has warned you to flee from the wrath to come? You too have to bear fruit if you would be acceptable to God. Don't content yourselves by saying that you have Abraham for your father. I tell you, God is able to raise up children to Abraham from these stones here. Right now the axe is laid at the root of the tree. Every tree that doesn't bring forth good fruit will be cut down and thrown into the fire.

PHANUEL *(To priests):* Ha, I guess he told you!

MALAK: This so-called prophet is insulting. I'm ready to fight him.

BEDEL: Be quiet, you fool. *(Stepping forward)* John, there is no reason for us to quarrel with you; we mean you no harm. After all, your father was a priest too. You seem to be doing a great deal of good. Only, tell us something about yourself. Who are you? People are saying you are the Messiah. I've heard that word whispered in the crowd today. Well, are you?

JOHN: I am not the Christ.

BEDEL: What then? Are you Elijah come to earth again?

JOHN: I am not.

BEDEL: Are you the prophet that Moses said would come some day?

JOHN: No.

MALAK *(Pushing forward, angry):* Who are you, then? Give us an answer so we can report to those who sent us.

JOHN: So you are spies from the temple. I supposed as much. Go tell your masters that I am the voice of one crying in the wilderness, "Make straight the way of the Lord," as the prophet Isaiah said.

MALAK: Then why are you baptizing if you are neither the Christ, nor Elijah, nor the prophet?

JOHN: I baptize with water, but among you stands one whom you do not know, even he who comes after me, the thong of whose sandal I am not worthy to untie. He will baptize you with the Holy Spirit and with fire. His winnowing fork is in his hand to clear his threshing floor and to gather the wheat into his granary, but the chaff he will burn with unquenchable fire.

JAPETH: Now can we be baptized? We are ready, John. We need cleansing.

PHANUEL: Yes, let's have an end to talking.

JOHN: Of course. If you are truly repentant of your sins, you may be washed in the river. Come one, come all of you.

DIAN: Just a minute, just a minute, John.

JOHN: Who is calling me?

DIAN: I'm the one. *(Emerges into center stage)*

JOHN: Oh, a daughter of Israel. What do you want?

DIAN: I need peace and forgiveness. I came today seeking help. But your words are so hard they frighten me. There is fire and destruction in all that you say. Is there any hope for me, any comfort for one whose sins are scarlet and whose life seems ended?

JOHN: I am sent in judgment to Israel to arouse men's hearts. You do not arouse men with soft words and easy promises.

DIAN: Then I am lost, lost, lost. *(Turns and walks slowly away)*

ADA: What a pity.

JAPETH: She is so young.

PHANUEL: He certainly isn't helping her.

JOHN: Wait, wait. *(Dian turns back)* I remember other words from the book of Isaiah. Listen: "Behold, the Lord God comes with might and his arm rules for him. Behold his reward is with him and his recompense before him." Now listen, daughter: "He will feed his flock like a shepherd, he will gather the lambs in his arms, he will carry them in his bosom, and gently lead those that are with young." Does that help?

DIAN: Yes, yes. God be praised.

JOHN: Then come, sister in the Lord. Be washed and find forgiveness and peace. Come, all of you. The Lord will cleanse you.

ALL: Hurrah! Praise the Lord! Into the Jordan!

(Exit singing the song with changed lines. Only MALAK *and* BEDEL *remain.)*

CROWD: He is John, John the Baptist,
John the Prophet of the Lord.
Let us go, go to Jordan.
We'll obey his mighty word.

MALAK: This man is dangerous. We must have him arrested.

BEDEL: No, Malak. This John is no threat to us. He will stir the people for a while, and then he will stub his toe. He'll fall on his face, and someone

else will oblige us by removing him from the
scene. But the other one . . .

MALAK: What other one?

BEDEL: The one who John says comes after him,
this gentle one who will be a shepherd to Israel.
He is the man we must fear. Bitter words are
soon forgotten. People aren't changed by accu-
sations. But love and forgiveness—ah, that's a different story. *(Businesslike)* Come on. Let's go back
to Jerusalem and make our report. *(Song continues
in the distance)*

Words and Music,
W. A. Poovey

1. There's a   man   in   the des-ert He is   preach-ing ev - ery day, He's a
2. He   is   liv - ing on lo-custs And sweet hon - ey ev - ery day, But his

proph-et of the Lord — So they   say, so they say. He is
words — they are bit - ter   So they   say, so they say.

Refrain:

John, John the Bap - tist , John the   proph-et of   the Lord. 1. Let us
2. We have
3. Let us

go, go   to hear him,   Hear his   might - y stir - ring word.
come,come to hear him,   Hear his   might - y stir - ring word.
go, go   to Jor - dan   We'll o - bey his might - y   word.

Housecleaning Time

Text: Mark 1:1-8

Housecleaning time! There was a day when those words sent shivers up and down people's spines. Housecleaning meant that heavy rugs had to be hauled outside and beaten, mattresses aired, curtains washed and stretched, and a dozen other unpleasant tasks faced. Today housecleaning isn't as strenuous in most homes, for modern fabrics and cleaning methods have eased the task. But the practice of periodically waging a war against dirt is still a good one, not only for homes but for lives. Dirt accumulates everywhere and needs to be removed.

The preaching of John the Baptist can best be understood as a call for housecleaning. This rough desert preacher came to stir a revival in Israel, to call on men to wash away the stains and ugliness of sin. His words were abrasive. His appearance was startling. But his whole ministry was aimed at mak-

23

ing Israel conscious of the need for cleansing and repentance.

The story of John's efforts is a fitting beginning for the Advent season, since Advent seeks to remind us of the need for housecleaning in our lives today. Being a Christian is no guarantee of permanent perfection or holiness for the believer. Unfortunately the daily events of existence have a way of soiling our lives and filling our hearts with ugliness. Selfishness creeps in. Lust rears its ugly head. Hatred and envy nibble at our righteousness. Because of our weakness, we cannot live in a dirty world and not get soiled by contact with others.

The Women's Chorus in T. S. Eliot's pray, *Murder in the Cathedral*, expresses the situation clearly:

> We are soiled by a filth that we cannot clean,
>   united to supernatural vermin,
> It is not we alone, it is not the house,
>   it is not the city that is defiled,
> But the world that is wholly foul.
> Clean the air! Clean the sky! Wash the wind!

This is the problem we face: how do you keep clean in a dirty world? We cannot isolate ourselves from life. Men have tried that. They have gone out into the desert or they have lived on some lonely island in the effort to escape the temptations of life. But all in vain. There is no escape from dirt. Only cleansing will purge our life from ugliness and sin.

The Bible constantly reminds us of that fact. It tells the story of many good and pious men, people like Abraham and David and Simon Peter and Paul.

But always there are unpleasant episodes in the lives of these people. David was an adulterer. Abraham a liar. Peter denied his Lord. Paul quarreled with his colleagues. We may think it would have been more kind to have omitted these unpleasant stories, but the Bible writers had a purpose in recording this material. Every description of weakness in the life of a godly man is a reminder to us that all men need cleansing.

And that is the message of John the Baptist. Repent. Wash. Be clean. John called the people of Israel to a "baptism of repentance for the forgiveness of sins." He spoke with boldness against evil wherever he found it, even when his words offended the ecclesiastical and civil authorities. And if his words have any meaning to us today, they should be heard as a clear call for us to clean house too. The Advent season should be a time for repentance, for soul-searching, for new resolves and new holiness.

Of course cleansing is not a once a year event for a man's heart any more than housecleaning should take place only on some special occasion. The Christian is to die daily to sin, that is, put away each day the evil that has crept in. But there is a need for special times of housecleaning, times for looking carefully at our lives and seeing what has happened to our high ideals. Such an effort can be very humiliating but also worthwhile. The Advent call to repentance is addressed to every Christian.

Yet there is a danger in housecleaning. A house is made to be lived in, and while it may be necessary to move furniture here and there for periodic scrubbing, it must all be put back so that life can be resumed. Otherwise the effort is a barren one. In one of his parables Jesus warns us against cleansing a heart and then failing to put something in place of the dirt. To drive out the demon and leave the heart empty is to invite seven other demons to move in and occupy the emptiness.

Cleansing our hearts at Advent then is important only when it is followed by increased love for our Lord Jesus. John the Baptist would have been a footnote in human history if he had not also been proclaiming the coming of the Messiah. His work was preparation, but it was preparation for a very special event. So it is the positive message that is important. The Lord draws near. The one who is mightier than John is coming. In harmony with this, we are to cleanse our hearts and lives so that we can be filled with the good news of the gospel.

Too often Christianity puts the emphasis on the negative, on the housecleaning. Men talk about the need to get rid of sin, or they measure their faith by the things that they don't do. The world's picture of a Christian is often that of a man who doesn't drink, smoke, swear, or tell dirty stories. But that's only the housecleaning side of our faith. Paul had the true picture when he spoke of Christ living in him so completely that the man Paul virtually ceased to exist. *That* is the Advent message. God has given us something better than dirt to fill our lives. He has given us Christ.

The Advent message sounds again today. It urges us to turn the searchlight of God's truth into the dark corners of our life and to cleanse each corner from the dirt that lies there. But the goal of Advent

is summed up in that little song most people learned
in Sunday School or Bible School:

> Come into my heart, come into my heart,
> Come into my heart, Lord Jesus.
> Come in today, come in to stay.
> Come into my heart, Lord Jesus.

DRAMA

Pamphlets and a Sign

MEDITATION

The Third Advent

Pamphlets and a Sign

SETTING

The setting is a typical middle-class living room. There should be several chairs and a table with a Bible on it. Also a waste basket. Other furniture is optional.

CHARACTERS

JACK CARVAN: retired, gruff, fanatical

MILDRED CARVAN: Jack's wife, a bit younger, mild in manner

DORIS CLAGGET: a middle-aged neighbor

STRANGER: tall, mysterious, changes voice and personality in play.

The stage is empty. JACK *comes into the living room carrying a sign which says, "Jesus is coming." If possible the entrance should be made down the aisle and onto the stage. He puts the sign down carefully, empties his pockets of pamphlets which he puts on a table beside the Bible. Then he sinks wearily into a chair.*

MILDRED *(Offstage):* Is that you, Jack?

JACK: Yeah. Who'd you expect?

MILDRED *(Appears in doorway):* Did you have a good day?

JACK: Nope. Rotten as usual.

MILDRED: Where'd you go today?

JACK: I walked up and down Main Street and Front Street. Then I went up and down the cross streets in between.

MILDRED: Lots of people down town?

JACK: Yeah. I'll bet I gave out over two hundred copies of my pamphlet, "Jesus Is Coming Now." But almost everybody who took a copy just glanced at it and threw it away. Didn't even get into a good argument with anyone today. Nobody seems interested in the end of the world or the Second Coming anymore.

MILDRED: I've been telling you that for a long time. Why don't you give up this business of "witnessing" as you call it and stay home and enjoy your retirement?

JACK *(Jumping up and his fanaticism shows):* No, Mildred, we've been all over this before. Even if I can't get a single person to listen, I'm doing my duty to warn people that they should get ready for the Lord. People may laugh at me and scoff at my pamphlets and my sign but I'll go on proclaiming the truth as long as the Lord gives me strength. *(He is shouting at the end and collapses into chair.)*

MILDRED (*Soothingly*): All right. All right, Jack. When you started this "witnessing" I promised not to nag you about it, and I'll keep my side of the bargain. But I hate to see you come home looking so tired and depressed. Maybe your sign is too heavy.

(*Picks up sign. He seizes it and puts it down carefully.*)

JACK: Leave it alone. It's not the sign. Things were just rougher than usual today. There was an old beggar who kept annoying me. I thought I knew all the panhandlers in town, but this was a new guy. Small and thin and a starved look about him. Everywhere I went he kept following me, begging for some money.

MILDRED: Maybe the man was hungry, dear.

JACK: Those beggars are all alike, Mildred. They just want money for booze. I gave him a pamphlet, but I don't think he read it. But he wasn't the only pest. There was a little girl over on Eighth Street. She was skipping rope and every time I walked past her house she grabbed me and tried to get me to jump rope with her. Can you imagine that?

MILDRED: I'd have enjoyed seeing you try it, particularly if you held on to your sign. But maybe you should have stopped and played with the little girl a few minutes. She probably was lonesome.

JACK: Mildred, you don't appreciate what I'm doing. I'm warning the people of this community to get ready for the Lord's return. I don't have time to play games with kids.

MILDRED: I don't think it would hurt you to relax and play a bit now and then.

JACK *(Abruptly):* I don't want to discuss it. Did we get any mail?

MILDRED *(Goes to table and comes back with letter):* Just one letter but it's an important one. It's an appeal for funds for Korean orphans. I think maybe we ought to send them a check. *(Offers letter.)*

JACK *(Refusing letter):* Mildred, you must be on every sucker list in the country.

MILDRED: But this sounds like a real needy cause. Here, read the letter. *(Offers it.)*

JACK *(Grabs it):* I don't have to read it. I know all these phony appeals. They work on people's sympathy and collect lots of money. Then the charity gets about 15 percent and the other 85 percent goes for salaries and overhead. *(He takes the letter and drops in waste basket.)*

MILDRED *(Exasperated):* Sometimes, Jack, you know too much for your own good. *(Sits.)* Or think you do. *(A knock at the door.)*

JACK: I'll get it. *(Goes to door.)* Oh, hello, Doris, come in. Mildred, Doris Clagget's here.

MILDRED: Why hello, Doris. Come in and sit down. I'll get another chair.

DORIS *(Just inside the door):* No, I haven't time. I'm on my way home to get dinner and I know you must be getting yours ready. I just thought I'd drop by a minute and see if you and Jack would like to go over and see Ann Linden tonight.

MILDRED: Ann Linden. Oh, she lost her husband about a month ago.

DORIS: Yes, and I guess she's pretty lonesome. I thought it might be nice if our two families could go and make the call together.

MILDRED: Why, that sounds nice. How about it, Jack?

JACK: You can count me out. Bill Linden was a scoundrel, and Ann Linden ought to be glad he's dead.

MILDRED: Why, what a thing to say!

JACK: Well, it's the truth. He never set foot inside the church, and he was a tight-fisted, mean old man. He used to stop me on the street and argue with me. Said he didn't believe in the first coming of Christ so how could he be expected to believe in the second one.

DORIS: I don't believe he was a very nice man, Jack. But all the more reason to go call on Ann.

JACK: I'm sorry. But I've got some studying to do tonight. A fellow gave me a tip on the meaning of a passage in the Book of Revelation. I've got to get busy and read it again. But you can go, Mildred, if you want to.

MILDRED *(Disappointed)*: No, I think I'd better stay home too, then. Sorry, Doris. Some other time, maybe.

Doris: Yes, some other time.

Jack *(Who had sat down, bouncing up):* Oh, before you go, Doris. Would you like a copy of my new pamphlet, "Jesus Is Coming Now"? Won't cost you a cent. Be glad to give you several copies if you want them *(Extending pamphlets).*

Doris: No thanks, Jack. My religion runs along more practical lines than yours. Good night, Mildred.

Mildred: Good night, Doris. (Doris *exits.)*

Jack: I wonder what she meant by that last crack.

(Sitting in chair) There's nothing more practical than planning for the second coming of the Lord.

Mildred *(Boiling):* I think I'll go get dinner, before I say something that will spoil our evening completely.

Jack: Hand me that Bible over there on the table, will you?

Mildred: Oh, get it yourself *(Exit).*

Jack: Hm. No accounting for women. *(Gets Bible, resumes seat and begins to study it. There's a knock at the door.)* I'll get it, Mildred. *(Grumbling)* Always somebody interfering when I want to study. *(Goes to door.)* Yes? What can I do for you?

Stranger *(Talks quietly, walks with a limp and is bent over):* May I come in a minute? I need some help.

Jack *(Ungraciously):* Well, come on in. What do you want?

STRANGER: My car ran out of gas right in front of your house. I wonder if you can help me?

JACK: Sure. There's a gas station about a half mile down the street. It's not a long walk.

STRANGER: I *am* a bit lame.

JACK: Not too lame to walk up to my door. You needn't worry. No one will bother your car while you go for gas. I'll even keep an eye on it for you.

STRANGER: You couldn't spare me a bit of gas, could you? Just enough to get to the station?

JACK: I've got no way to get it out of the tank. Besides, why should I give you free gas? And I don't want to sell it to you. Might get into trouble that way.

STRANGER: So you might, so you might *(Defeated)*. Well, thanks for the information at least.

JACK: Oh, no charge for that. By the way, here, take one of my pamphlets, "Jesus Is Coming Now."

(Takes pamphlet from desk.) It'll do you good to read it. It'll make you realize the importance of making preparations for the Second Coming. Might even make you check up to see that you have enough gas in the tank.

STRANGER *(Takes pamphlet):* Thank you. You are a Christian, then?

JACK: Oh, yes. Been one all my life. Only recently got interested in the Second Coming though. Greatest doctrine in the Bible. And all the signs point to this being the time of the end. One of these days, very soon, the skies are going to open and the trumpet is going to sound and Jesus is going to appear with the armies of heaven. And those who aren't ready for him will sweat for it. Mark my words, they'll sweat for it. It's all in the pamphlet. You read it, stranger, and if you're ever back this way again, I'll be glad to explain it all to you in greater detail.

STRANGER: Thank you. You are very kind—about some things. And now—(*The* STRANGER *straightens up and his voice changes. There is the roll of thunder or perhaps the blare of a trumpet.*) maybe you'd better sweat for it, Jack Carvan. Down on your knees, man. And listen to me for a change.

JACK (*In terror*): Who are you? What do you want of me? (*Falls on knees.*)

STRANGER: I am just who you think I am. I'm the one you are expecting to come from heaven with a mighty conquering army. I will come that way, someday. But not yet, not yet.

JACK: Not yet, Lord?

STRANGER: Not yet. But I do come to people on this earth every day and every hour. You saw me to-day again and again, but you failed to recognize me.

JACK: Lord, I didn't see you. I swear I didn't.

STRANGER: Oh yes, you did. I was the beggar who

asked you for help, but you passed me by. I was the little girl who was lonesome and wanted someone to play with, but you were too busy toting your sign around to stop and cheer me up, even for a moment. I was the orphans who needed your money, but you were too wise to recognize a cry for help. I was the widow Linden who needed the comforting presence of friends, but you were too filled with venom because her husband had scoffed at your ideas. And I was the motorist to whom you gave a pamphlet when what he needed was gas for his car.

JACK: But I didn't know, Lord. I didn't know.

STRANGER: That's what men will tell me at the last day. "When did we see you hungry or thirsty or naked or sick or in prison?" Do you remember the rest or have you buried yourself so deep in your fantasies that you remember nothing else from my Word?

JACK: I remember, Lord.

STRANGER: Then take heed. *(Slowly.)* You're a wicked man, Jack Carvan, for all your prating about the Second Coming. But there is mercy even for you. Only remember, those who do not see Christ in their fellow man will not see me with joy when I return in power.

JACK: Mercy, mercy, Lord. Have mercy on me. *(Exit* STRANGER.*)* Mercy, mercy. *(Looks around.)* Why, where is he? Where has he gone?

MILDRED *(Entering):* I heard the door close. Who was here? And what are you doing on your knees, Jack?

JACK (*Rushing to her*): Mildred, Mildred, I saw him. I saw him. He was here, right in this room.

MILDRED: What are you talking about, Jack Carvan? Who was here?

JACK: The Lord Jesus. I thought he was a stranger wanting gas for his car, but it was the Lord himself. And he was the beggar and the little girl and the Korean orphans and Ann Linden.

MILDRED: That does it. I've had enough of your religious nonsense. Now your brain has finally snapped. Here. Let me at that sign. (*She seizes it and tears it apart.*) You're not going to parade around the streets again with that stupid sign. And you're going to throw away all those silly pamphlets you have stored around the house. Here, I'll get rid of these myself. (*Throws pamphlets into waste basket.*)

JACK (*Calmly*): Thank you dear for getting rid of that stuff. If you hadn't done it, I would have.

MILDRED: Do you mean it?

JACK: Yes, I mean it. I guess I can't explain to you what happened here tonight, but maybe you can understand this. Call Doris Clagget and tell her we'll go see Ann Linden tonight. And before we go, fish out that letter from the waste basket and make out a good check for those Korean orphans.

MILDRED: Oh, it's good to hear you say that! You really must have had a wonderful visitor to make you change like this.

JACK *(Fervently):* I did.

MILDRED: But I won't be satisfied until you promise you won't go parading around the streets again with pamphlets and a sign.

JACK: I'll promise that. But tomorrow I'm going back where I was today. Maybe I can find a beggar who needs money or a little girl who would like to skip rope.

The Third Advent

Text: I John 4:19-21

Where is Jesus Christ today? Where can we find him? Is there any place in this world where a man can meet his Lord face to face? In a confused and confusing society, that isn't an idle question. We need Jesus. We need to feel close to him. But where is he?

The obvious answer is that Jesus is *not* to be found. He has gone away. In the words of the Apostles' Creed, "He ascended into heaven, and sitteth on the right hand of God the Father Almighty." Unfortunately we are between the two Advents. We know that there was a time when Jesus Christ lived on this earth. We believe there will come a time when he will return. But we are caught between the times, born too late or too soon.

Fortunately, that's not all the answer. The Word of God speaks about a different kind of presence of Jesus, Our Lord promised his disciples and his church, "Lo, I am with you always, to the close of the age." He declared, "Where two or three are gathered in my name, there am I in the midst of them." But even more striking is Jesus' assertion that he is always to be found among the poor, the needy, the unfortunate in this world. "I was hungry . . . I was thirsty . . . I was a stranger . . . I was naked . . . I was sick . . . I was in prison." Jesus in the great judgment scene recorded in the Gopel of Matthew says that if we want to find him, we should seek him among those who need help. This is a kind of third advent, a daily coming of Jesus Christ into men's lives through the appeals of those in need.

It should not be surprising that Jesus chooses to be where the poor are. After all, at his first advent men criticized him severely for his association with lepers, blind men, fallen women, the unfortunate refuse of society. The charge levelled against him was, "This man receives sinners and eats with them." Jesus never denied the accusation; he simply insisted that the well do not need a doctor, the sick do.

Thus the answer to our original question is very simple. Jesus today is just where he always was— among those who need him most. If we would come close to him, we must seek him there. Perhaps the most significant line in the play is spoken by Jack Carvan when he says of Christ, "He was the beggar and the little girl and the Korean orphans and Ann Linden." Jesus Christ is mankind in need.

Translated into contemporary terms, we can say that Jesus can be found among rebellious youth, among black militants, among people on relief, among old people living on inadequate pensions, among the lonely, among those who seethe in rebellion in the prisons of this nation. Is it any wonder that so many in our society fail to find Jesus today? They wall themselves off from their fellow men; they shut their ears to the cries of the needy and the unfortunate. How surprised such people are going to be on Judgment Day when they hear their Lord declare, "Truly, I say to you, as you did it not to one of the least of these, you did it not to me."

But there is still something puzzling here. How can the good and holy Jesus be found among the lowly in our society? We have learned through bitter experience not to be romantic about the poor, the lonely, the prisoners. To be unfortunate is not necessarily to be good. We know that people in jail may often receive harsh treatment, but they can also be brutal and ugly in their words and deeds. We have come to realize that oppressed minorities can turn on their oppressors and exhibit the same kind of mindless violence that they have suffered. The poor can be lazy, the old can be ungrateful. The beggar who asks money for food may spend any donation for liquor. How can Jesus be found among such people?

Once again the answer is shown in Jesus' first coming. Why did he come at all? Was it because we were such noble people? Because man deserved a savior? Not at all. Jesus came because he saw the potential in man. He saw what man could become. In Simon Peter Jesus saw a man who wasn't a rock but could become one. The woman at the well in Samaria wasn't a very nice person but Jesus saw she could be a missionary to her own village. In Saul, the persecutor, the Lord could see Paul, the great leader in the Gentile church.

In other words, Jesus Christ saw the Christ in

everyman. He believed that men could become little Christs, beings who could truly call God Father. Jesus believed his own statement that a man can be born again and can become a new creature through that birth. The poor, the weak, the sinful seem the farthest from God, but they have the same potential possessed by all men.

Jesus asks us to see that potential too. Men are not noble, kind, forgiving, loving, or peaceful by nature, but they can become that. Everyone of us has that same possibility. We have been made in the image of God, and although that image is marred by sin, it can still be restored through God's grace.

In the early part of this century Robert Haven Schauffler wrote a poem entitled "Scum o' The Earth" that reflects this truth. The poem describes the immigrants who come to our shores and who are often maligned by scurrilous nicknames. One verse describes the Jewish immigrant and ends with the words:

> Man—lift that sorrow-bowed head.
> Lo! 'tis the face of the Christ.

That's what we are to see in the scum of the earth, in the poor, the ugly, the weak. The potential for goodness is there. We face Christ everywhere. We must see him in every human being.

But what happened to the text we read? What has all this to do with John's statement that if we cannot love our brother whom we have seen, how can we love God whom we have not seen? Actually the text fits the material very well. For in a deeper sense, John is saying that if we cannot see God in our brother, we cannot see God at all. Or to put it in the words of John A. T. Robinson and John, the author of this epistle:

> Whether one has "known" God is tested by one question only, "How deeply have you loved?"—for "He who does not love does not know God; for God is love."

DRAMA

The Bride

MEDITATION

Tired of Waiting?

The Bride

SETTING

A modest living room. Three chairs and a table are all that are needed but other items of furniture can be added if desired. A window on one wall is useful but can be imagined at the front of the stage. Only one exit needed although a second is helpful.

CHARACTERS

Lois: young girl, dressed in a bridal outfit

Clara: the mother, rather soft and easily led

Matilda: the aunt, sharp, crafty, but able to conceal these qualities

As the scene opens, Clara *and* Matilda *are seated on either side of stage, reading or sewing.* Lois *enters, dressed in her wedding gown. She parades before each of them, showing off her gown.*

LOIS: How do I look? Mother? Aunt Matilda?

CLARA: You look beautiful dear, simply beautiful.

MATILDA: They say all brides look beautiful so don't feel too complimented, Lois. Especially since you aren't a bride yet.

LOIS *(A bit hurt)*: I don't really care what anyone thinks of me except Chris. I do want *him* to think that I'm beautiful when he gets here.

MATILDA: *If* he gets here.

CLARA: I'm sure he'll be here eventually, and he'll think you're beautiful, Lois, dear. But do you really think you ought to be all dressed up like this? You aren't sure when he will arrive.

MATILDA: Or whether there'll be a wedding when he does arrive.

LOIS: You two might as well be quiet. He told me in his letters that I should always be ready for him. Keep a close watch, he said, so that I don't surprise you. Here, let me read his very words to you.

(Picks up packet of letters from table.)

MATILDA: Oh no! Not those letters again. You've almost worn them out, reading them to us. Spare us the letters.

LOIS: All right. But I never get tired of reading Chris' letters. They're the only things that keep me alive and waiting for him. The letters and the remembrance.

CLARA: What do you mean, the remembrance?

MATILDA: Did he give you some special gift? Where is it? Why haven't we seen it?

LOIS: Don't get so excited. Chris hasn't given me anything except his love. But you remember how we used to walk along the river before—before he went away?

MATILDA: We remember all right. Sometimes we thought you'd never do anything except walk with him.

LOIS *(Sitting down):* I suppose that's the way it seemed to you. But it was a very special walk for us. We usually sat on a bench beside the river and talked about the world and people. When Chris went away he told me to walk down that same road often and sit on that particular bench. He said I would remember him if I did that.

CLARA: How romantic!

MATILDA: Sentimental nonsense. *(Disgusted, gets up and goes to window.)*

LOIS: Perhaps. But I've done it many times and I *have* remembered him, just as he said I would. It's as if he were there with me. Only of course the remembrance is no substitute for having him in person. But he'll soon be here. I'm sure of it.

MATILDA *(From window):* You may be right. A man just went past the house and he looked for all the world like Chris.

LOIS *(Runs to window):* Where, where?

MATILDA *(Pointing):* See that man disappearing around the corner—

LOIS: Oh, it does look like him. It must be him. I'll go call him. *(Starts for exit.)*

CLARA *(Seeks to hold her back):* Lois! You can't go out there like this. Stop, stop.

LOIS: No, no. Let me go. I must find Chris. *(Exit, calling)* Chris, Chris.

CLARA: Now you've done it, Matilda. You know that wasn't Chris out there.

MATILDA: *Do I? (Sits in center chair.)* Lots of people look like Chris. Maybe one of them will turn out to be him.

CLARA: That's mean, Matilda. *(Sits in left chair.)*

MATILDA: Well, she's a silly little goose—always ready for Chris, she says. But he's not ready for her. He's not coming back. You know that and I know it. It's time Lois faced up to the facts of life.

CLARA: Matilda, we don't know he isn't coming back.

MATILDA: Where is he then? We've waited and waited. His letters promise that he'll return, but nothing happens. I say it's time we stop this foolishness, this waiting for a lost bridegroom.

CLARA: Oh dear, it seems so hard.

MATILDA: Clara, you've got to face facts. Lois will never be reasonable and practical until we cure her of this obsession. We've got to make her forget

Chris and settle down to a normal life in this world.

CLARA: I suppose you're right. But how can we do that? You know how she idealizes him.

MATILDA: I'm aware of that. And that's the clue to what we must do. We've got to convince Lois that she's not good enough for Chris. You let me start, and then you back me up.

CLARA: It seems a cruel thing to do to my own daughter.

MATILDA: Clara, I don't see how you ever managed to raise Lois at all. You have to be hard with young people. This obsession with Chris must be ended. Now you've got to help.

CLARA: I suppose it's for her own good.

MATILDA: Of course it is. I think I hear her coming back. Remember, back me up.

CLARA: All right. (*Lois enters. She is crying and her grown is in disarray.*) Come in, dear. It wasn't Chris, was it?

LOIS: No, it wasn't. Oh I feel so humiliated, so unhappy.

MATILDA (*Very sweet*): I'm sorry I misled you dear. Tell us what happened.

LOIS: The man you saw did look something like Chris from the back. I hurried after him and called him but he didn't stop. When I caught up with him I pulled his arm . . .

CLARA: And . . . ?

LOIS: It wasn't Chris at all. The man's face was evil. He leered at me and said, "You want to talk to me, girlie?" Then he grabbed me and tried to kiss me.

CLARA: How awful!

MATILDA: How odd. No one tries to kiss me. Maybe I should try grabbing strange men now and then.

LOIS: Don't joke about it, Aunt Matilda. I had to run most of the way home to escape that evil man. And it's all my fault. I should have known better.

CLARA: I did tell you not to run out in the street wearing your wedding gown.

LOIS: I don't mean that. But Chris warned me that while he was gone some people might come around and pretend to have messages from him. He even said some might try to claim they were him, but that I shouldn't be fooled. He said I would know him when he came back, no matter how long he stayed away. Here. I'll show you in one of his letters—

MATILDA: Again, spare us the letters, my dear. But while you were gone your mother and I have been talking about Chris and we think there are some things we three should discuss together. As a family. Sit down here and let's have a talk.

LOIS (*Sits in vacant chair*): If you two are going to try to convince me to forget Chris simply because he's been away a long time, you might as well save your breath.

MATILDA: We wouldn't try to do that, dear. Chris is a dear, wonderful boy and we all love him very much.

LOIS: I like you better when you're sharp and hard, Aunt Matilda. What are you up to now?

MATILDA *(On her feet):* Nothing, my dear. But did it ever occur to you that Chris might not want to marry you when he returns? Or at least that he might not want to if he knew the truth about you?

LOIS: What do you mean? Chris love me.

MATILDA: He loves what he thinks you are. But suppose he saw you with your hair up in rollers. Or with your face dirty. What then?

LOIS: I tell you, he loves me.

MATILDA: But did he ever see you lose your temper? Or catch you telling him a lie?

LOIS: Why are you asking me such questions?

MATILDA: Because someone has to serve as your conscience. And because Chris is a good clean decent boy who wants his bride to be perfect all the time. And you're not. *(To Clara)* For heaven's sake, help me a little.

LOIS: I try to be good.

CLARA: Not always, Lois, dear. *(Stands up.)* You did leave the dirty dishes in the sink yesterday after telling me you were going to do them. *(To Matilda)* Is that okay?

MATILDA *(To Clara):* That's a start. Now let's pour it on. *(From now on they advance like two furies on Lois.)* You lost your temper and swore at me last week.

LOIS: But you were so exasperating!

MATILDA: Of course I was. I always am. But that's no excuse for you.

CLARA: And you didn't go with me to visit Mrs. Casper when she was ill.

LOIS: But she's such a bore.

MATILDA: Exactly. Chris would have urged you to go. but you only want to do the things that please you. You don't think of others.

LOIS: That's not so. At least—

MATILDA: The truth of the matter is, Lois, that you're not good enough for Chris.

CLARA: Not nearly good enough.

MATILDA: You see. Your own mother tells you you're not good enough for him. And those precious letters that you've gotten from Chris. You've read them so many times. But have you forgotten how often he told you in his letters to be good while he's gone? Isn't that what the letters say?

LOIS: Yes, yes.

MATILDA: I even remember one where he told you to be good to *everyone*.

CLARA: That's right. Good to everyone.

MATILDA: And especially to those in your own home. He did say that, didn't he?

LOIS: Yes, he said it.

CLARA: He also told you to help out the poor people in this community. Have you done that?

LOIS: I've tried! I've tried!

MATILDA: But not hard enough. There are still lots of poor people that you've never even visited.

LOIS: I can't do everything!

MATILDA: But Chris expects you to do everything. He wants his bride to be perfect.

CLARA: That's a hard word—perfect. But that's the kind of person Chris is.

MATILDA: I tell you, you're not good enough for him. *(They stare in her face.)* Tear up those letters and forget him.

CLARA: Tear them up.

LOIS *(Breaks away):* I won't! I won't! Oh you've both got me so mixed up.

MATILDA *(At table):* Here are the letters. If you don't destroy them, I will.

LOIS *(Seizes them):* No, no. Let me look at them again. Then maybe—just maybe—I'll destroy them. Here's one of the first ones he wrote to me. *(Opening letter.)* "Dearest Lois, love and peace to you. I hope you are showing your love to everyone while I am gone."

MATILDA *(Triumphantly):* You see, you see.

LOIS *(Reading):* "Remember, I love you. I have always loved you. I loved you even when you scorned me and rejected me when we first met."

CLARA: You never said you rejected him. Ever.

LOIS: But I did, to my shame. I was very mean to him. *(Reading.)* "I will always love you, not because you are good and kind, though you are. I love you because you are you. You are my darling Lois." *(Begins to laugh and continues to do so. Turns back on audience.)*

CLARA: What are you laughing about?

MATILDA: The girl's hysterical. Slap her face. She's having a fit.

LOIS *(Whirls around):* No, I'm not. You can slap my face a hundred times but I'll still laugh. Oh Chris, to think that I almost let them get away with it.

CLARA: What are you talking about?

LOIS: Simply that you thought you could make me give up Chris by convincing me that I'm not good enough for him.

MATILDA: You're not, you're not.

LOIS: Of course I'm not. I never was and I never can be. Chris knew my weaknesses right from the start. He knew I was proud and foolish and deceitful and careless and whatever else you want to accuse me of. He saw my bad temper and my ugliness when I rejected him at first. But he loved me. That seems impossible for you to believe. It's true! It's true! He loves me! And he always will. And I'll wait for him if it takes a thousand years. Someday the knock will come at the door. And when I open it, Chris will stand there with arms open to receive me and I'll be with him forever and ever. *(A knocking begins at the door. Lois runs toward the door. Clara and Matilda stare. Blackout.)*

Tired of Waiting?

Text: John 3:1-3

Nobody likes to wait. The husband standing on the corner while his wife completes her shopping is filled with apprehension and impatience. The author, wondering whether his manuscript will be accepted, feels that the postman will never arrive. Children thinking about Christmas find that each day seems a week long. Waiting is no fun. The man who said that anticipation is better than realization never had to wait for anything that he really desired.

Unpleasant though it may be, however, you and I have to wait. We have to wait for Jesus Christ. The whole history of the Christian church can be summed up in that one word—waiting. Someday, the Scripture promises us, our Lord will return. Advent season is a time set aside for stressing Jesus' return as well as his first coming. But Advent seasons come and go. Generations pass and he does not come. And we wait.

Each time we join in the Apostles' Creed, we say, "He shall come to judge the quick and the dead."

Each time that we come to Holy Communion we are reminded that we show forth the Lord's death—until he comes. In many passages the Bible speak about our Lord's return. John writes, "When he appears we shall be like him, for we shall see him as he is." There is no *if* he appears, but *when*. Deeply imbedded in almost every book of the New Testament is the simple truth—Jesus shall return. And we wait.

But that's a bit of an exaggeration. Most Christians don't wait. The Second Coming of Christ is one of the most neglected teachings in the Bible. It is a teaching which has become the playground of the sects and fanatics. Yet every Christian is dimly aware that without this teaching we have a very unsatisfactory faith. To equate the good things which God promises with the things which we have at present in this world is a poor fulfillment. Every believer hopes for something better—a better world free from war, pain, and suffering. Thus, whether we clothe our words in the classical form of the doctrine of the Second Coming or not, we want what it promises. And still it eludes us.

Perhaps it will be worthwhile to review just what the Second Coming of Christ involves. Too often we are caught up in the mechanics of it, concentrating on the trumpet blast from heaven, the great day of judgment, or the nature of life eternal. But when we sift it all down, the Second Coming means that someday Christ will be with his church again in a very real sense. He was here once. He promises to return. It's as simple as that. There will no longer need to be any Holy Communion to bring us close to him. There will no longer need to be any Bible to serve as a collection of letters from him. Jesus Christ will be with us.

And his presence will bring joy to his church. The Bible several times uses the figure of a wedding to describe the Second Coming. We are invited to a marriage feast, to a great Messianic banquet. The church is called the bride of Christ, and the bridegroom will come for his bride. The figure is a fitting one. No bride in love with her husband-to-be thinks that his absence is better than his presence. And the church, even though it has many blessings now, knows that the present cannot compare with the future. John catches this thought in the text by insisting that we are already the children of God, but that there is something indescribably better ahead. The bridegroom will return, and joy will be complete.

But how do we know he will come? Waiting can be a fruitless experience sometimes. The exected guest fails to show. The check in the mail never arrives. How do we know that Jesus will return? The answer is a simple one: the bridegroom has promised. There was no doubt in John's mind, for he had heard the promise. Peter believed that "the Chief Shepherd" will be manifest, for he had heard Jesus' promise to return. The first Christians received a solemn assurance at the Ascension, "This Jesus who was taken up from you into heaven will come in the same way as you saw him go into heaven."

The Christian church therefore has no cause for anxiety. Jesus Christ has promised, and he keeps his promises. No one can explain why we must wait so long, of course. But it should be noted that the first coming of Christ also seemed long delayed. Sometimes we skim through all the Old Testament material so quickly that we forget the long years covered by these events. Men became impatient then, and some lost hope that a Messiah would ever come. One of the psalmists cries out in desperation, "Oh that deliverance for Israel would come from Zion." But only when the time was ripe did the Savior appear. Even though almost twenty centuries have passed since the promise was made, we must cling firmly to the certainty that Jesus will return. He has promised.

Waiting can be deadly when there is nothing to do in the meantime. Pacing the floor in a waiting room can be terribly boring. Sitting on the sidelines, hoping for the big play, can frustrate us. Fortunately the Christian is not left with idle time on his hands while he waits. "Occupy until I come," says the man in the parable of the pounds, and this is our Lord's advice too. The whole Bible is filled with instructions of what to do while we wait. Keep busy. Do the Lord's will. Let your light shine. Feed the hungry, clothe the naked. So the words run. John sums it up by saying we are to purify ourselves, and that isn't an invitation for introspection, but for service. Anyone who accuses the Bible of being other-worldly, of taking man's mind away from day by day living to a future "someday" simply hasn't read the Scriptures.

But how much easier it makes the tasks in this life when we remember that there is something better ahead. The traveller shivering through the winter remembers the spring. The workman carrying the heavy load knows that there will come an

end to the day, and that there is a good meal at
home. The Christian knows that same kind of comfort. We wait. But we wait for something wonderful, for the return of the bridegroom. Someday we
will hear the knock at the door. And then we shall
see him and be with him.

FOURTH SUNDAY IN ADVENT
I PETER 1:10-12

DRAMA

From Heaven Above

MEDITATION

The God Who Doesn't Lie

From Heaven Above

SETTING

The setting is the office of DARCI, one of the High Councilors of Heaven. There is a desk, a small typewriter table,
a drawer with file cards, and several chairs. The furnish-
ings do not need to be grand. Characters may wear ordi-
nary clothes or may be dressed in robes. No effort should
be made to provide wings or haloes. DARCI should have a
more impressive costume than the other two.

CAST

MARTA: a secretary, efficient but inclined to plot and
scheme

DARCI: a leader in Heaven, a bit amused at MARTA

GAYLUS: a newcomer from the earth, polite and humble
in attitude

OFF-STAGE VOICE

*As the scene opens, choir music is heard, rather loud. MARTA
is fiddling with some cards. The music dies down a little
so we can hear MARTA's lines. Music should be a familiar
hymn; a portable phonograph can be used. DARCI or
GAYLUS can be the voice off stage if desired.*

MARTA: Oh, that choir again. I don't know why they keep on practicing. They're always perfect the first time they run through a number. Everything's perfect here in heaven. It's too perfect. Nothing ever seems to happen except for the arrival of a few immigrants now and then from some out of the way place in the universe. And this office has to keep a file on every one. Here I am, talking to myself again when I ought to get on with my filing. But how can I with that choir always singing in my ear? *(Yelling at them)* Say, will you be a bit quieter out there! I'm trying to do some work.

OFF-STAGE VOICE: All right, sister. Sorry to disturb you. *(Singing fades.)*

MARTA *(Yelling):* That's better. Everybody's so polite around here. Only now I don't feel like working at these filing cards. *(Voices off stage.)* Oh, oh, I hear Darci. He mustn't see this pile of cards. *(Hides them)* Maybe he'll have some exciting news.

(DARCI *enters. He looks a bit downcast and weary.*)

MARTA: Hello, Darci. Council meeting over already?

DARCI: Yes. *(Sits on chair.)*

MARTA: I wish you could take me along to the meeting sometime. Even though I'm not a High Councilor of Heaven, I'd like to hear for myself what goes on at one of those meetings. Your reports are usually too brief. Get everything settled?

DARCI: Yes, Marta.

MARTA: You don't sound too happy about things.

DARCI: I'm not.

MARTA: Can't you be a little more talkative? You know I always want to hear about the discussions and what the council decided.

DARCI: Marta, you could worm secrets out of the Lord himself. I suppose I might as well tell you the whole story. The council didn't decide anything because it was all decided and cut and dried before we got there. But the news will rock the galaxies when it gets out.

MARTA: Tell me, tell me quickly! I'm dying to hear the latest. Only I don't suppose dying is the right word to use in Heaven.

DARCI: Well, to put it in a nutshell—the Son has decided to leave.

MARTA: Oh, is he going on another trip? I wish I could go someplace sometime. There's a strange happening occurring right now out at the edge of things. They say a whole new universe is being born. I suppose the Son is going out there to see what's going on. I'd like to see it myself.

DARCI: Marta, you don't listen when I *do* tell you the news. I didn't say anything about a trip. I said the Son was leaving.

MARTA: Leaving? Leaving for good? Is that what you mean?

DARCI: Not really for good. But he's going to be gone for a long time. And he won't be the same when he comes back.

MARTA: But that's terrible. What's happened? Has there been a quarrel? Surely not that!

DARCI: No, nothing like that. I suppose I might as well tell you the rest of it or you'll get it all mixed up and mislead all your friends with your wild exaggerations. *(Steps to edge of stage.)* Come over here.

MARTA: To the edge?

DARCI: Yes, to the edge. (DARCI *holds on to* MARTA. *She is frightened.*) Now look down there. *(They peer out.)* Can you see that collection of stars called the Milky Way?

MARTA: You mean that fuzzy, cottony cloud way out there?

DARCI: Fuzzy, cottony cloud! Oh my. That's the one I mean. Now look at the star close to the edge of the galaxy. Can you see it?

MARTA: Of course. My eyes are as good as yours.

DARCI: All right. Now look at those planets moving around that star.

MARTA: You mean those spinning colored balls? I see them.

DARCI: Your astronomical descriptions are delightful. Now if you count out from the center, you come to the third of these "spinning colored balls." That ball is called the earth.

MARTA: The earth! So that's where the earth is. I've heard about it because every now and then someone from the earth comes up here. Not very many of them, mind you, because the earth seems like a terrible place. But I've never really known where it is. Geography of the universe isn't my strongest suit.

DARCI: I'm aware of that. Better step back from the edge before you learn some of that geography first hand. *(They resume former positions.)* Well, Marta, that small spinning ball happens to be where the Son is going.

MARTA: No! It can't be. Why the earth is a terrible place. Full of sin and wickedness, so I've heard.

DARCI: You've heard right, this time. But my news is even worse. The Son is not only *going* there, he's going to *live* there. He's going to be born into a human family just like all the rest of the inhabitants of the earth. He's going to grow up like any earthling, and when he's grown he's going to try to teach the people there what they should know and do.

MARTA: But this is incredible. How will it all turn out?

DARCI: I don't know. There's still some mystery about it. When we asked him he looked pleased and sad at the same time, but he didn't tell us any more.

MARTA: Darci, this is awful. The Son can't do that. Didn't the council tell him he shouldn't go?

DARCI: Of course we told him that. Every member of the council tried to discourage him. Earth's reputation is pretty widely known here, you know. But all our efforts meant nothing.

MARTA: But you should have pointed out that there are millions of worlds in the universe, and if there aren't enough he can always make more. It isn't fair for him to waste time on one little world like that.

DARCI: Marta, I don't think even your highly imaginative mind can think up any arguments that we didn't use. We tried all the persuasion that we could, but he simply smiled, thanked us, and said he had to go. And the Father backed him up. Apparently they have been planning this for a long time. And there is nothing we can do to prevent it.

MARTA *(Begins to walk the floor)*: Oh yes, there must be something. The trouble with you councilors is that you give up too easily. There must be a way to keep the Son from making such a terrible mistake. And I intend to do something about it.

DARCI: Oh, oh. Here we go again. Just what do you have in mind?

MARTA *(Pacing the floor)*: Well I—no, that won't work. Did you try—no, that's no good. Say, I have it. Were any representatives from earth there?

DARCI: No. They're not members of the council. You know that.

MARTA: Then there's the answer. The people who come up here from the earth tell perfectly terrible tales about conditions down there. What we have to do is bring those stories to the attention of the Son.

DARCI: Don't you suppose he knows all about what goes on there?

MARTA: It's not the same as hearing it from someone who's been there. We've got to get hold of someone who's come up recently. Say, what was the name of that man who was assigned to our division a few days ago?

DARCI: Just a minute. I have his card right here. *(Searches through cards.)* But it'll never work, Marta.

MARTA: It's worth a try.

DARCI: All right. *(Searching.)* Marta, where are the rest of the cards?

MARTA *(Guiltily)*: I'm sorry. I didn't get them all done so I hid them. *(Retrieves the cards.)*

DARCI *(Mock seriously)*: I might have known. *(Takes cards.)* Loafing on the job. Labor troubles even in heaven. *(Finds card.)* Here it is. Gaylus. Room 242.

MARTA: Please call him in. I'm sure he can do us some good.

DARCI: This sounds like another of your wild schemes. Anyway, don't you think we would do better to get one of the old faithful crowd from there—Abraham or Joseph or—I have it—David. The Father always liked David.

MARTA: No, no. Those older fellows only know what earth used to be like. We need the last word on conditions there. Please call Gaylus.

DARCI: Oh, all right. *(Goes to door.)* Send Gaylus from room 242 here immediately.

OFF-STAGE VOICE: Gaylus. Gaylus to the councilor's office.

MARTA: Now you let me talk to him. This is *my* plan.

DARCI: The pleasure is all yours. Ah, I hear him coming. We do get good service here anyway. Come in, Gaylus.

GAYLUS *(Entering):* Thank you. I hope there's nothing wrong, sir. I just arrived last week.

DARCI: No, no. Nothing wrong at all. But my secretary, Marta, wants to talk to you. She thinks you might be able to help her.

GAYLUS: I'll be happy to do what I can.

DARCI: Good. You may proceed, Marta.

MARTA: Thank you. Gaylus, I have a very special reason for asking my questions so don't think I'm being impertinent. I know you've just come from the earth, so will you tell me what conditions were like down there when you left?

GAYLUS: Oh, terrible, terrible. The whole world is full of wickedness and my native land, Israel, is the worst of all, I'm afraid.

MARTA: Beautiful. Beautiful. Tell me what's wrong with Israel?

GAYLUS: Well, the Romans are in charge there. They're cruel and arrogant and they've bribed some of my countrymen to help them do their dirty work.

MARTA: How lovely. Are the Romans the only problem?

GAYLUS: Oh, no. They have put a man named Herod in charge of the land and he's a monster, a liar, a lecherous beast, a—oh there are no words in heaven or on earth to describe him. But even that's not the worst. The religious leaders in Israel are corrupt, wringing money from the people and strutting around in pride and arrogance. They observe little details of the law, and at the same time they hate and mistreat the people they're supposed to serve.

MARTA: Oh, it couldn't be better.

GAYLUS: Better! You mean it couldn't be worse.

MARTA: Yes, yes, that's what I meant of course. Gaylus, would you be willing to tell some high officials what you've just told me? Would you be willing to speak to—the Son himself?

GAYLUS: Oh, I couldn't! The very thought frightens me. Why would you want me to do a thing like that?

MARTA: I suppose I can tell him?

DARCI: It can't do any harm. Everyone will know it soon enough.

MARTA: Well, Gaylus, the Son himself has just informed the council that he intends to go down to your vile little earth. He intends to live there, to be a real inhabitant of the earth for a time. He has some crazy dream that he can help the people there. But I'm sure when he hears your report . . .

GAYLUS *(Walking to the edge of stage):* So, it's come at last. The time that the prophets talked about. O blessed be the holy one of Israel!

MARTA: What? What are you talking about?

GAYLUS: The time that the prophets told us about. But they never dreamed that God himself would come to earth.

MARTA: I don't understand. I don't understand at all.

GAYLUS: I'm sorry. I'm so overjoyed that I simply didn't make myself clear. You see, earth has always had troubles. Men have sinned and defied God and wandered in darkness. But always there have been some men among us who talked of better days. They told us that God had not forgotten his world, that someday he would send a redeemer to us. The redeemer is to be a prophet like Moses, a king like David, a priest like Melchizedek. Isaiah told us that he would be a wonderful counsellor, a prince of peace. It's been these prophecies that have kept our hopes alive. Sometimes we have grown discouraged and then in the darkness God has sent us another prophet who has raised our heads again. And now, now it's all to come true.

MARTA: Then you won't speak to the Son and try to discourage him from going?

GAYLUS: Discourage? When I think of poor suffering people down on that little earth so far away—I could wish I were back there to see and hear their joy when their Savior comes. I wonder, sir . . .

DARCI: What is it, Gaylus?

GAYLUS: Could I be excused so that I can go and tell others who are here from the earth that the great day is near, the day of redemption. They'll make the very walls of heaven ring with their shouts of joy.

DARCI: You may go, Gaylus. Thank you for coming.

GAYLUS: Good day to you both. *(Exit.)*

MARTA: Well! That was a boo-boo. But how was I to know?

DARCI: Marta, Marta, will you never learn? The Son does not make any foolish or idle plans. And you should have known this scheme wouldn't work. A man may think his homeland is a terrible place, but he still loves it and wants it improved, not destroyed.

MARTA: I suppose you are right. Well, I'll just have to come up with another scheme, I suppose.

DARCI: Surely you're not going to continue this foolishness.

MARTA: You're too easily discouraged, Darci. There must be a way to prevent this whole foolish plan, and I'm going to find it. Let me see—ah, I have it. A petition.

DARCI: Oh no! Not a petition again. Marta, in the past five years you've drawn up and presented 26 —no 27 petitions. And you haven't had one approved yet. Remember how you petitioned to have comets outlawed because one flashed past your bedroom window one night? And remember your petition to have all angel wings painted yellow to match the gold in the streets? Then there was the one about . . .

MARTA: Don't remind me of my past failures. This time I intend to succeed. Yes, I think a good petition will do the trick. I believe I could get a million signatures asking the Son to remain here. That should impress him.

DARCI (*Sarcastically*): A million is a nice round number.

MARTA: Well, that's my goal. First, let's see what I want to say. (*Paper in typewriter or can be done in longhand.*) I suppose the petition should begin with the statement that we all love the Son and don't want him to leave. (*Typing or writing.*)

DARCI: I think he's already aware of that fact, Marta.

MARTA: Nevertheless, it makes a good beginning. Then maybe I should put in something about the bad conditions on the earth—without any corroborating testimony from earthlings this time. *(Typing or writing.)*

DARCI: I see you've learned your lesson about the people from the earth.

MARTA: O I have, I have. I don't even want them to find out about the petition until it's all finished and presented to the Son. I guess I ought to include something about all the other worlds in the universe and the need for concern for them. *(Typing.)* And then I'll conclude with an appeal from all heaven's loyal subjects to ask the Son to change his mind. I think that's the best I can do. *(Typing.)* Now, Darci, you can be the first to sign my petition. *(Offers it to him).*

DARCI: So nice of you. Thank you for the honor. But I'm afraid I'll have to refuse. You see, there's just one little thing I forgot to tell you about all this.

MARTA: What? What did you leave out? It may be important to include in the petition.

DARCI: Just this. The Son happens to love the inhabitants of that small spinning ball called earth. Every time we tried to argue with him he said, "But I love those people down there." Have you taken that fact into account?

MARTA: He—he—loves them?

DARCI: Yes. And the Father loves them too. You see he made them, in his own image.

MARTA: Darci, you deliberately led me on. There goes my petition. *(Tears it up.)* And all my opposition. You don't argue with God's love. Even I know better than that.

DARCI: Nice try, anyway.

MARTA: Darci, I'll never interfere again. I've learned my lesson.

DARCI: Don't make foolish promises. Even in heaven there has to be one like you. And now I have a surprise for you.

MARTA: What now? If it's a pleasant one, I could use it.

DARCI: Well, when the Son is born on earth there is to be an announcement made. And you're to be one of the choir singers. I volunteered your services.

MARTA: Oh, oh, you know I don't like choirs. Still, it might be nice. Will we sing in the king's palace or in the great temple in Jerusalem that Gaylus told me about last week?

DARCI: I'm afraid not. You're to sing to some shepherds outside the city of Bethlehem.

MARTA *(Deflated):* I might have known. Well, I hope we get lots of practice. I don't want to sing off key and upset the sheep. Still, when I practice, I have a pretty nice voice. *(Vocalizing.)*

DARCI: Marta. The file cards, please. First the file cards. Then the vocalizing.

The God Who Doesn't Lie

If you take a look at the Bible, you will note that most of it is what we call the Old Testament. There are more books and longer books in that section of the Scriptures. And, it must be added, *stranger* books. Indeed, the world of the Old Testament seems very foreign to us. Here are stories of giants and judges, of warring nations, and of strange people and customs. Some of the material seems very primitive and bloodthirsty to our modern ears. It is not hard to understand why there have always been men in the church who have advocated jettisoning the Old Testament and retaining only the New.

But if the Old Testament had no other value, we would still find it helpful for one purpose: it shows us a God who does not lie. The Old Testament is the record of God's faithfulness despite man's almost continual rebellion. Dominating these ancient books is God's clear promise that he would not desert his people. Indeed in book after book God promised through his prophets that he would send a redeemer for all men.

It must have seemed an idle promise when God told Abraham that he would bless all people through his family, particularly when Abraham didn't have any family. No wonder Sarah laughed. Yet the prophecy was fulfilled. It must have seemed to the children of Israel that God was a liar when he left them as slaves in Egypt. Yet God sent a Moses. It brought bitterness into men's hearts when God's people were in captivity in Babylon. One can hear the anguish in the psalmist's voice when he sings: "By the waters of Babylon there we sat down and wept when we remembered Zion." Yet God returned a remnant of his people to their homeland. For God does not lie.

Of course Jesus Christ is the supreme example of that truth. As Peter points out, men in Old Testament times talked again and again about the redeemer who should come. Many times men examined these prophecies to try to understand just who this redeemer would be and when he would come. In Jesus Christ God made good his promises. He does not lie.

Most of us however may be tempted to ask, "So what else is new?" We are not inclined to doubt God's Word, at least in theory. The pagans had gods who lied and stole and were often worse than the people who worshiped them. But we have no such problems today. If all these prophecies do is show that God does not lie, we don't need them. God in our eyes is a gentleman who keeps his word.

What is remarkable however is the "how." Faithful Israelites didn't doubt God in Old Testament times either, but they found it difficult to understand just what was going to happen. The character in the play who expresses amazement that the Son of God would come to earth to redeem mankind certainly is in harmony with the prophets. They knew that somehow God would do it, but the method was beyond their comprehension.

We can even feel a little sympathy for the people in Jesus' day who found it hard to accept his claims. They had dreamed of a royal rescuer, a great king who would defeat their enemies. When the Messiah turned out to be a humble man from Galilee, a man who had been born in a manger and had grown up as a carpenter, many found this hard to take. That he claimed a peculiar relationship with God didn't make his acceptance any easier. The "how" in the story is enough to shock an angel.

Really, God's way of keeping his word is always strange. "My thoughts are not your thoughts, neither are your ways my ways," God declares and we can all say amen to that. He picks out a people for his own who are small and unimportant and who prove to be stiffnecked and difficult. God sends his son to live in an obscure land, no bigger than San Diego County in California. He lets that son be rejected and finally crucified. The methods of God are as puzzlesome today as they were for the prophets. We find it hard to believe even when we read it all in the Bible. God doesn't lie but he certainly uses strange methods to make good on his promises.

But there is a clue to all this. The key to the Advent story and to the prophecies is not just honesty. Sometimes people try to use the prophecies to prove that the Bible is true. But we misunderstand if we think that Old and New Testaments picture God as an honest business man who uses strange methods but makes good on his guarantees. The issue is deeper than that of truth or lying. The real key is love.

God keeps his word because he loves man. *He loves man.* That truth finally broke the back of Marta's plotting in the play. It will shatter the opposition of every man who truly reads the Bible with an open mind. For the Bible is a love story. It's the story of a God who will not give up, who shakes off all of man's rebuffs and who persists in his efforts to bless us. Again and again Israel failed God and came under the threat of his punishment but God's true nature appears in the Book of Hosea when in the midst of bitter words God says, "How can I give you up, O Ephraim? How can I hand you over, O Israel?" God's love never wavers.

Moreover, this is a purposeful love. It is not some romantic, sentimental concern. God wants to restore man to his rightful place in the universe, for man was made in the image of God. And all heaven and earth will be shaken in an effort to bring man salvation. The story is so amazing, so overwhelming that we need the entire Bible to convince us of the truth of this love by God. One example of God's concern will not suffice. We need the broad sweep of history to convince us that this God loves.

Thus the Advent message is not just a call to repentance. It is also a call to respond to love. The

Lord of the universe woos us. The Son of God stands humbly before the door of our heart, seeking entrance. We dare not refuse the great lover—God. He is the Hound of Heaven, the persistent suitor, the God who does not lie, but loves.

What's It All About?

Text: Luke 2:8-14

What's it all about? What's Christmas all about? Ask a small child and he may say, "It's about toys and candy and vacation from school." Ask a postman and he may reply wearily, "It's about letters and packages and sore feet and a strained back." We all have our private views of what Christmas is all about. But there are truths that go beyond our private joys or annoyances, truths that are of the essence of Christmas itself. What's it all about?

It's about God. Christmas starts with God. No human being dreamed up this story. We can imagine things like Santa Claus and elves at the North Pole. Men can write stories like "The Gift of the Magi," which tells how a wife sold her hair to buy a watch fob for her husband while he pawned his watch to buy her a beautiful set of combs. But only God can send a Savior to be born in a manger and dispatch angels to announce the event to shepherds.

These shepherds couldn't have missed the point.

101

"The glory of the Lord shone around them," we are told, and the angels highlighted their message by singing, "Glory to God in the highest." Unfortunately no angel voices assault our ears, and no heavenly light shines around us. And it is so easy for us to get involved in the affairs of this life and thus miss God's part in Christmas.

But we dare not let that happen. Christmas is about God. It's about a God so moved by love and so concerned about man that he intervenes in human affairs. The first Christmas gift came from God. And in this holy season our first thought must be thankfulness for what God did for us.

But it is a mistake at Christmas to get too involved in the supernatural. Christmas is about men, all men. The events of Christmas took place on this earth. The whole story is centered in humanity. It concerns a woman and a baby, and you can't get closer to this earth than that. Christmas is about a heathen king and a census, a crowded inn and some shepherds on a hillside. There is an earthy air to all of this.

Unfortunately we are always tempted to embroider the story, to magnify the unusual in Jesus' birth. Artists who paint pictures of the nativity sketch heavenly rays of light emanating from the baby, and few painters can restrain themselves from including angels and cherubs hovering overhead. Old legends say that at midnight the cattle knelt before the newborn child, and that they continue to do this each Christmas eve. With the best of intentions, men try to lift the whole story out of its earthly setting. But this is all wrong.

For the message of Christmas is about men. God's Son comes to earth to show God's concern for men.

And part of that concern lies in complete identity with men. The fact that the announcement was made to shepherds underlines this point. Had the angels appeared to the High Priest or to Herod's court, we would have reason to doubt. But to shepherds—that says it. If such men are involved, we are all involved. Christmas is about men.

What's it all about? One simple word says it— Savior. Christmas is about a Savior. The appeal in that word moved the shepherds to go to Bethlehem. The prospect of seeing a newborn child, even one lying in a manger, would not have challenged them. But a Savior—that is a different story. The old Wakefield mystery play catches this note when the first shepherd reacts to the angel's announcement by saying, "This was as sweet a sound as every yet I heard." The word "Savior" catches at the heart.

It still has an intriguing sound. Man today also needs a Savior. All our human cleverness seems in vain. We move from crisis to crisis. Our scientific progress only seems to create greater problems. Our new freedoms bring no happiness. No matter what remedy we try, it doesn't seem to work. We are in the same situation as the spirits in Dickens' *Christmas Carol:* "The misery with them all was clearly that they sought to interfere for good in human matters and had lost the power forever." The power to help seems gone from us too.

But a Savior. Someone to lift us up. That's what the world needs, and we are beginning to realize it. This is the unique message of Christianity. Help has come for men. No wonder the angel told the shepherds that this was good news of a great joy. We are in a better position to grasp that than the shepherds were. We know this child grew to be a man who gave his life to redeem us. In a world bowed down by problems, the word "Savior" has a wonderful ring.

There is one final word in the angelic message that needs emphasis. Christmas is about peace. "And on earth peace." How that word intrigues and yet mocks us! Think how many Christmases men have spent at war with their fellow men. Think how often peace has eluded human beings in their relationships with one another. Think how many this Christmas are at war with themselves or are seeking momentary forgetfulness in drugs or alcohol. There is almost a mocking ring in that beautiful word *peace*.

And yet the pattern for peace was clearly marked out on that first Christmas. The child in the manger was Christ the Lord, but he had laid aside all his majesty to be born on this earth. His life was a sacrifice from beginning to end. He brought peace by yielding all in love. And this is the way of peace for men today. Nations fight because they cannot lay aside their pride or their greediness. Men struggle because each wants his own way. Human hearts are filled with bitterness because they refuse to love.

The way to peace is still open today. God indicated that way by giving his all to men. And Christmas calls on men to follow the pattern by letting love replace selfishness in each heart. In the words of Christina Rosetti:

> Love came down at Christmas,
> Love all lovely, love divine.
> Love was born at Christmas,
> Stars and angels gave the sign.

What's it all about? Christmas is about life for all men. It's about a God who loves us all. It's about a Savior who yielded all. It's about peace that comes through love. That's what it's all about.

DRAMA

What Kind of a Savior?

MEDITATION

Light in the Darkness

What Kind of a Savior?

SETTING

The stage is bare except for a few rocks. These can be low stools, covered with cloth. CALEB and OLAS sit on the rocks; MITAN and SARDEN stand during the play. MITAN and OLAS are at opposite ends of the stage, downstage. CALEB upstage, SARDEN in the middle. Use simple shepherd costumes. Men should have staves.

CHARACTERS

CALEB: the grandfather

SARDEN: the father

MITAN: the older son

OLAS: the younger son, a teenager

VELDA: a young woman

SARDEN *(Looking around):* It's a clear night. *(Finger up to test wind.)* No breeze. And no noise from the sheep.

CALEB: Yes. It *is* quiet. Just like it was on that *other* night.

MITAN: It was just about a year ago.

SARDEN: Almost to the day. Or night, I suppose I should say.

OLAS *(Standing up):* Don't you three ever think about anything except that night? You *keep* talking about it.

CALEB: Grandson, I'm close to my three score and ten. And on only one night of my life has an angel spoken to me. Why should I forget such a night?

MITAN: You keep thinking about it too, Olas. Only yesterday you were arguing with me about the place where the angel appeared. And you were wrong.

OLAS: I was not. *(Pointing.)* It was right over there where those bushes are. That's where we all first saw the light where the angel appeared. Isn't that so, father . . . grandfather?

MITAN: It wasn't there at all. It was more to the left. I remember seeing the light hit that colored stone there. *(Pointing.)* I'm sure that's the place. Isn't it, father?

OLAS: He's wrong. I saw the light hit those bushes. Just because you're three years older, that doesn't mean you're always right. I *am* right, aren't I, father? *(Both face father.)*

SARDEN: Won't you boys stop arguing and grow up? I don't know what difference it makes just where the light appeared. I'm sure I can't remember. I was too scared when it happened. Just like the rest of you were.

OLAS: I wasn't afraid. Maybe I was surprised for a minute. But I wasn't afraid. *(Bragging.)*

MITAN: Oh no! Your teeth were still chattering when we got to Bethlehem.

OLAS: That's not so. Is it, father?

SARDEN: Another argument?

CALEB: Of course you were frightened, Olas. And why not? Anyone who isn't frightened by an angel, much less a whole choir of them simply hasn't got good sense. I was frightened, and I've faced lions and wolves in my day.

OLAS *(Defeated):* I guess you're right. I was scared, just like the rest of you . . . but I've been wondering. We only made one trip to Bethlehem. Why haven't we been back to visit the child and his mother? They're still there.

SARDEN: That's right, they are. Somebody told me that Joseph—I think that was his name—has set up a carpenter shop there.

MITAN: We ought to go again. It's late but we could go back this very night and see them again.

CALEB *(Standing up):* We'll do nothing of the kind. We were sent the other time. The angel made it clear that we should go. But nobody told us to be regular visitors.

SARDEN: You're right, Caleb. If the child is really to be a Savior as the angel said, he doesn't want a crowd of shepherds visiting him all the time. He'll need more important people than us around him.

OLAS: Then why were we supposed to go in the first place?

CALEB: I'm not sure. Not sure at all. Still, not everybody would go to a *stable* to see a new born savior. Even angels couldn't make some people take such a trip. So maybe we were just the kind of simple people to believe a story like that. *(Sitting.)*

SARDEN: Well, we weren't disappointed when we did go. Only, ever since that night I've been doing some thinking. I've been wondering what kind of a Savior that baby is going to be when he grows up.

OLAS: Oh, I can tell you that.

MITAN *(Sarcastically):* I was sure that you would know.

OLAS: It's not hard to figure out unless you're stupid. What do we need to be saved from? The Romans, of course. They've got soldiers everywhere in this land, making us pay taxes and carry their stuff around and obey their slightest command. *(Mocking)* "Jew dog, carry my pack. Jew dog, move along. Jew dog . . . " Oh, how I hate them.

CALEB: Easy, easy, boy. They're men just like we are.

OLAS: That's my point. They're men, not gods. What we need in Israel is a leader who can beat them at their own game, and drive them out of the land. I think this baby will be a warrior, just like king David was. When this Savior grows up, he'll raise a big army and defeat the Romans just like David beat the Philistines. And I'll still be young enough to help him. *(To Mitan)* Ho there, Roman dog. I'm going to kill you. *(Shakes stick.)*

MITAN: The likes of you won't kill anyone. *(Uses his stick. There is a little struggle.)*

SARDEN: Will you boys stop your nonsense! You'll wake up the sheep and then we'll have our hands full. *(They stop.)* Besides, Olas, I think you're wrong. This Savior isn't going to bring peace by killing a lot of people. And even if he is going to do that, he won't need your help. He'll have all those angels to do his work for him.

MITAN: Of course he will. At least if he wants to win, he shouldn't rely on a soldier like you.

OLAS: No no? I'll bet you I get an important place in his army. I don't intend to be a shepherd all my life. I'm going to tell him that I was one of those who visited him when he was a baby in Bethlehem. That ought to help me get an important job. *(Sitting.)*

MITAN: If you're right about the Romans being the enemy, that *might* help. But I don't think he'll be that kind of king at all. It's not the Romans who are the real enemy. It's work and not having enough to eat that plagues us.

SARDEN: What do you mean, son?

MITAN: Well . . . look at Grandfather Caleb.

CALEB: Me?

MITAN: Yes, you. All your life you've had to work hard. You've told us that enough times. And what do you have to show for it—nothing. Every day you simply have to do the same things over— watch the sheep, guard the lambs, fight off any wild animals that come around. And you'll keep on doing that until you drop.

CALEB: Maybe that day isn't too far away.

SARDEN: Father! Only God knows that.

MITAN: But what I'm saying is how much nicer it would be if we didn't have to work. If we had a Savior who would see to it that we had enough to eat and a place to sleep and some fun in between —why that would be paradise again. The Romans could run the government if they wanted to. I couldn't care less.

OLAS: Why, you traitor to Israel. *(Grabs at him.)*

SARDEN: Olas, behave. You had your say. Now let Mitan finish. *(Olas sits again.)*

MITAN: There's not much more to say. I just want to be saved from work and from always having to struggle for something to eat. I'd like to lie down on this hillside and take a nap every afternoon. And I'd like to be sure there was something to eat when I got home, even if I didn't work every day. *(Lies down.)* That's my idea of a real Savior.

OLAS: That's not right, is it father? That's not what the Savior will be like?

SARDEN: I don't really think so, Olas. I'm afraid Mitan has let his natural laziness color his view of what a Savior should do.

OLAS: Ha, ha. Lazybones. *(Pokes at him with his stick.)*

MITAN: All right. So I don't like to work. It would be nice to have a Savior do the things I said, but I suppose that's expecting too much. *(Sits up.)* But Father, if I'm wrong and Olas is wrong, what's right? What do you think this Savior will be like?

OLAS: Yes, suppose you tell us.

SARDEN: I'm not sure. But the angel talked about peace, and I've been wondering if the whole story isn't in that one little word.

CALEB: But Sarden, there's no war going on now. We don't need a Savior to stop wars that aren't even happening.

SARDEN: No armies are fighting now. You're right. But that's not exactly the kind of peace that I mean. People are *always* fighting with one another. Even Olas and Mitan can't get along half the time. And you know how the shepherds on this side of Bethlehem are always quarrelling with those on the north side of town about the pasture land.

MITAN: Old man Jardis is always fighting with his wife. He gave her a black eye the other day.

SARDEN: Exactly. Everywhere you look people are quarrelling, fighting, getting angry, or getting hurt. There's no love, no feeling of being human beings together. It's Jews against Samaritans, Pharisees against Sadducees, priests against common people. Everywhere, trouble and struggle. That's why I hope this Savior can save us from all that. If he can bring some love into the world, if he can teach men to live together in peace, I'll be satisfied.

CALEB: That's a beautiful picture, son. If you're right, I hope I live long enough to see it happen.

OLAS: But grandfather, you haven't told us what you think about this Savior. Do you agree with father?

CALEB: I don't know. I'm still thinking. Maybe we'll just have to wait and see. I . . .

MITAN (*Has been listening*): Quiet. I hear a voice. (*They all listen.*)

OLAS: I'll bet it's a wolf attacking the sheep. (*Grabs staff.*)

MITAN: No, it's off in that direction. And it's no wolf. It's someone calling for help. Listen. Listen. (*Faint cries.*)

CALEB: Someone is running this way. I can hear the rustle in the grass.

MITAN: It might be a trick. Someone may be planning to attack us and steal our sheep.

OLAS: I've got my stick ready. Just let somebody try to attack me. (*On the defense.*)

SARDEN: Over here. We're over here.

MITAN: You're leading them right to us.

SARDEN: It's a woman's voice. Over here.

VELDA (*Appears carrying baby wrapped in blanket*): Help me! Help me! Don't let them catch me. (*Runs and hides behind* CALEB.)

CALEB: Young woman, what are you doing out in the wilderness at this time of night? And with a baby in your arms. You'll both catch your death of cold.

VELDA: Hide me, hide me. Don't let them take my baby!

OLAS: Who's chasing you? You're safe here. I'll protect you. (*On guard.*)

SARDEN: We'll all protect you if you need protection. Now what's this all about?

VELDA: It's Herod's soldiers. They're after me.

CALEB: Now look here, young woman. Is this some kind of a joke? There aren't any soldiers here.

SARDEN: She's too frightened to be joking. Catch your breath and then tell us what the trouble is.

VELDA: You'll not betray me? Can I really trust you?

SARDEN: Of course you can. But we've got to know what the trouble is.

VELDA: If I tell you, will you hide me from them?

SARDEN: My dear young woman, if you need a place to hide, I'll take you to my wife, and she'll hide you so that a hundred soldiers will never be able to find you. Now, tell us your story. And start from the beginning. Who are you? Where do you come from?

VELDA: I live in Bethlehem. My name is Velda and my husband died several months ago. He never even got to see our baby. But shortly before he died, some new people moved next door to us, into a little broken down house there. The man is a carpenter named Joseph. He's a newcomer from Galilee. I don't suppose you know him.

MITAN: We know him. And his wife Mary. And they have a baby.

VELDA: Well, that makes it easier to explain if you know the people. I got acquainted with them as soon as they moved there. Mary was so good to me when my husband died and later when my baby was born. Still, she seemed a bit strange, as though she knew a great secret and couldn't tell anybody about it. Then, just a few nights ago they

had peculiar visitors in the house—very odd looking people dressed in rich robes. After they left I
tried to get Mary to talk to me about them but
she can be very close-mouthed when she wants
to be.

MITAN: An unusual woman.

CALEB: Quiet, Mitan. All this doesn't explain what
you're doing here.

VELDA: I'm coming to that. Despite their strange-
ness, I felt I was lucky to have good neighbors
like Mary and Joseph. Then tonight it happened.
My baby was cranky and I couldn't sleep. Otherwise I wouldn't be here and neither would my
baby. You see, in the middle of the night I heard
noises next door and when I peeked out I saw
Joseph loading all their clothes and things on to
the donkey. Then Mary came out with the baby
and they started out. Apparently they were leaving
Bethlehem without telling anybody where they
were going.

OLAS: Leaving Bethlehem! Then we'll never get to
see them again. Unless you found out where they
went.

VELDA: I did try to find out. Their leaving like that
seemed so strange so I snatched up my baby and
ran after them. I could see them in the distance,
but I was scared to call out to them, and when I
got outside the city, they were gone.

MITAN: How odd! First angels and now this.

VELDA: What?

SARDEN: Nothing. Tell us the rest of your story. How did you get *here?*

VELDA: Well, when I lost sight of them, I started back to Bethlehem. And just as I got close to the city, I was almost run over by a crowd of soldiers on horseback.

OLAS: Romans?

VELDA: No, I think they were Herod's men, though I only got a glimpse of their uniforms.

OLAS: Herod is no better than the Romans.

MITAN: I don't think you should say that.

OLAS: Well, I said it. Herod is a traitor.

SARDEN: Must you start a political argument in the midst of this woman's story? What were the soldiers doing in Bethlehem?

VELDA: That's what I wanted to know. I started to walk after them. They had stopped in front of a house on the edge of town. I crept closer and heard the leader say, "Remember, seize every baby boy in the town."

SARDEN: No! That's hard to believe.

CALEB: What won't Herod do next? Is that why you came here?

VELDA: Yes. That was enough for me. I simply held my baby close to me and ran and ran.

MITAN: But the baby next door to you? Mary's son? He's safe?

VELDA: I think so. They left just before the soldiers arrived. But barely.

CALEB: Thank God, at least *they're* safe. What a terrible business!

(Noise off stage.)

VELDA: What was that?

SARDEN: What do you mean?

VELDA: I heard a noise. Oh, I'm so afraid. There. There's the noise again.

SARDEN: It's only the sheep. It's getting close to dawn, and the sheep are beginning to stir.

VELDA: Are you sure that's all it was?

SARDEN: Yes, I'm sure. A shepherd knows the sound of his own sheep. But you're too frightened to stay out here any longer. I'll take you to my home, and you'll be safe there. Come with me.

VELDA: Thank you. I didn't expect to find such kindness. Never again in this world.

SARDEN: Come. *(They exit.)*

OLAS: Well, that does it. Herod seizing babies. And our so-called Savior doing nothing about it.

CALEB: Olas, he's only a little baby.

OLAS: I don't care. Somehow he ought to have done something. If I'd have been there, I would have fought those soldiers. They wouldn't have grabbed any babies.

MITAN: They would just have had one more baby to deal with.

OLAS: Why you—oh, I won't stay here and argue. I'm going after father and that girl. Maybe I can help her. It doesn't seem like I'll ever be able to help that so-called savior now. Hey, wait for me.

(Exit.)

MITAN: Well, grandfather, I guess we're left to take care of the sheep. And I'm the one who doesn't like to work. It's been some night.

CALEB: Yes, it has. And wouldn't you know, now that the rest are gone I think I've figured out what kind of Savior that young baby is going to be.

MITAN: Tell me, tell me, even if the rest aren't here.

CALEB: All right. But first, take a look. The daylight is beginning to glow in the east. Things that we couldn't see in the dark are beginning to grow plainer. I think that Savior is going to be like the dawn. He's going to shine and make things clear that have been dark. He's already made Herod show what he's like. And just thinking about him made you reveal your laziness and Olas his blood-thirstiness. And your father showed his love for peace.

MITAN: That's right.

CALEB: I think that's what this Savior will do to every man. Those who want to serve God will get that chance. He'll make it come about. And those that want to do wicked things—the light will drive them deeper into the darkness. He'll be a Savior but only for those who want to be saved. That's my prediction. But now we can only wait and see.

MITAN: Yes, grandfather. Wait, and tend sheep.

Light in the Darkness

Text: John 1:4, 5

There is an interesting parallel between the first book of the Bible and the opening verses of John's Gospel. Genesis starts with the sweeping statement "In the beginning God . . . " John begins with the words, "In the beginning was the Word." The third verse of Genesis describes God as saying, "Let there be light; and there was light." The fourth verse of the Gospel, speaking about Jesus says, "In him was life, and the life was the light of men." In both instances light comes from God and penetrates into the darkness, the chaos of the world.

But there is a difference. In the Genesis account God speaks, and it happens. He is in complete command. The majesty, the power, the sovereignty of God controls events at the beginning of time. But Jesus does not command. He provides light, but does not force men to accept that light. He offers, but he does not insist.

Many people wish that the two accounts were completely parallel. They would like to see God force his will on men, make them obey his command. They see Jesus as a weakling, not a Savior. If he is good, why doesn't he stop all wars? Why doesn't he make everybody be kind? Why doesn't he kill all disease germs and heal everyone immediately? Such people want the light to overpower the darkness. They would like God to be a puppetmaster, who pulls the strings and makes men dance to his tune.

Such a view fails to note the difference between the book of Genesis and the Gospel of John. When God said, "Let there be light," he was dealing with matter, with atoms and electrons and energy in his universe. But Jesus Christ came to bring light to human beings, to creatures made in the image of God, creatures still retaining the power to act and react. Thus God allowed Herod to use his own power to kill or not to kill. The characters in the play each had the power to decide what kind of a Savior he wanted or believed in. The light from Jesus Christ is never blinding or compelling. It is inviting, but men do not have to yield to it. The atheist, William Ernest Henley who insisted, "I am the master of my fate, I am the captain of my soul," was reflecting the truth, even though he spoke in defiance of God.

Yet, when we say that the light that comes from Jesus Christ is not the powerful, overwhelming light of Genesis 1, we are not casting aspersions on the nature of Jesus. He does not force men to do his will, but he *does* make us react. The minute he appeared on the scene, men were forced to accept or reject his claims. They could not remain neutral. Nor can we today. The Bible knows of only two classes of people: the children of God and the children of darkness. The light must be faced. Man must decide where he wants to stand.

This decision making is a continual process. Every day we are forced to decide for or against the light. We go to church, and we come out either better or worse—never the same. We are constantly challenged by opportunities to do good or to refuse to act. We either go forward, or we slip back into the darkness. For this is the nature of the light that comes through Jesus Christ. It constantly confronts us with an either/or.

However, it isn't profitable to concentrate too much on the darkness. Christmas and Epiphany are times to stress the light. The observance of Epiphany has some relationship with the old pagan customs at the winter solstice, when the sun seemed to return and the days began to lengthen. The word "Epiphany" means manifestation, the showing forth of the light from God. Among Eastern Christians January 6 was time for stressing the baptism of Jesus, among Western worshippers the day marked the coming of the Wise Men. But in both areas Epiphany has always meant a stress on the light from God shining into the darkness of this world.

And that is what Jesus Christ is: A light in a darkness, a leader who has come to show us the way. Think for a moment what life was like in this world before Jesus came. Darkness certainly was in control. Only a handful of people understood the real nature of God. Few had any hope of eternal life. If God was honored at all, men thought of him as a stern ruler who punished but did not love. Of course there were many who longed for a better way of life, but they simply did not know where to turn for help.

Look at the world today. Darkness is still powerful. Millions do not yet know Jesus Christ. But the
light from God has shined into the world, and the
darkness has not overcome it. No longer do men have
to face death with a stoic resignation to the inevi-
table. They can now know death as victory. No
longer do people have to wonder whether God is an
enemy or a friend or perhaps the Great Unknowable.
Men can know God through Jesus Christ. The worshippers of the true God are not limited to a handful in one little land. The light has shined into almost
every part of the globe. If men want to serve God,
they now have that chance, as the grandfather in
our play predicted they would. The light is here.

No one can calculate all the changes that have
taken place as a result of the birth of Jesus Christ.
But we are right to measure our time by that event.
For the coming of the light has changed the whole
course of human history. The light mentioned in the
first chapter of Genesis made the whole universe
possible. But the light of the first chapter of John
made real living possible. John weaves together life
and light in his Gospel. He has caught the right note.
For Jesus Christ has penetrated the darkness of our
existence and given us true life.

The dramas in this book are also available in a separate volume, *Let Us Adore Him: Dramas for Advent, Christmas, and Epiphany.* No performance fee is required providing a copy of the play is purchased for each player.